THE PERFECT APPRAISAL

Howard Hudson is an Independent Training Consultant, specializing in helping people develop their management and interpersonal skills.

Before going freelance in 1988, Howard was employed with British Airways in the 1960s, an Industrial Training Board and Hogg Robinson Travel through the 70s, then OXFAM during the 80s. His extensive practical experience of Personnel, Training and Line Management has led to his becoming a leading Consultant in the fields of: Recruitment and Selection, Appraisal and Staff Development, Employee Relations, Teambuilding and Leadership, Effective Meetings, Customer Care, Time Management, Assertiveness and Presentation Skills. His consultancy and training assignments to date have included work with organizations as diverse as British Nuclear Fuels, Forte Hotels, Philips Electronics, Pearl Assurance, The John Lewis Partnership, NHS and Friends of the Earth.

OTHER TITLES IN THE SERIES

THE
PERFECT
APPRAISAL

All you need to get it right first time

Howard Hudson

RANDOM HOUSE

BUSINESS BOOKS

3 5 7 9 10 8 6 4 2

This edition published in the United Kingdom in 1999
by Random House Business Books

First published in 1992 by Century Business
Random House, 20 Vauxhall Bridge Road, London SW1V 2SA

Random House Australia (Pty) Limited
20 Alfred Street, Milsons Point
Sydney, New South Wales 2061, Australia

Random House New Zealand Limited
18 Poland Road, Glenfield
Auckland 10, New Zealand

Random House South Africa (Pty) Limited
Endulini, 5a Jubilee Road, Parktown 2193, South Africa

Random House UK Limited Reg. No. 954009

Papers used by Random House UK Limited are natural, recyclable
products made from wood grown in sustainable forests. The
manufacturing processes conform to the environmental regulations
of the country of origin.

ISBN 0 09 940626 8

Companies, institutions and other organizations wishing to make
bulk purchases of any business books published by Random House
should contact their local bookstore or Random House direct:
Special Sales Director
Random House, 20 Vauxhall Bridge Road, London SW1V 2SA

Tel: 0171 840 8470 Fax: 0171 828 6681

www.randomhouse.co.uk
businessbooks@randomhouse.co.uk

Typeset in Sabon by SX Composing DTP, Rayleigh, Essex
Printed and bound in Norway by AIT Trondheim AS

To
Julie, Simon, Neil and Daniel –
who are forever appraising me, perfectly

Contents

Foreword

I well remember having my first appraisal. At the age of twenty-five, I was told by my manager that I was too old to change career path. 'You stick with what you know', he advised. Within a year I had resigned to do the very thing he had advised me not to.

If I had taken my manager's advice, this book would never have been written. Mind you, in a way, it is precisely because of what he said that I have written it. For, in my book, The Perfect Appraisal is all about managers helping each of their staff achieve the exact opposite of 'sticking with what they know'. It is about the two of them regularly meeting to discuss what they can learn from the past to help create a better future. Looked at in this way, appraisal becomes an integral part of managing work and people in concert – matching the goals of the organization with those of individuals, to create a 'best fit'.

Two more things arise from this. First, this book is all about how to prepare for, conduct, and follow up the joint discussions which are at the very heart of The Perfect Appraisal. In some appraisal schemes:

- Managers can get away with simply filling in forms on their staff – and do not even have to show them what they have written, let alone talk to them about it, if they choose not to.
- Staff can get away with keeping their heads down and their noses clean – and do not even have to take an active part in their appraisals if they do not want to
- Both can therefore get away with paying lip service to the appraisal process – if it does not work for them

Not in The Perfect Appraisal, they can't. For it firmly places responsibility on them both to get together regularly to talk about work – and to work out what is best for them and their organization. It becomes **their own** scheme – and what is offered here is a detailed framework for constructing this.

Second, although not all appraisal schemes are based on managers conducting appraisals with individuals – for example, in team and peer appraisals – this is the most common scenario and the one taken here. It can also be the most difficult one to handle well, as it involves putting the spotlight on two people and their working relationship, in a situation of unequal status – sensitive issues at the best of times.

This then, quite simply, is what The Perfect Appraisal is about. Not that it is necessarily quite that simple to accomplish. For it does involve discussing assessments of people's performance, giving and taking criticism as well as praise, referring to weaknesses as well as strengths, talking about limitations as well as future potential and, in some cases, even encouraging certain people to see that their future lies elsewhere. **And** it is about doing all this in a way that everyone finds acceptable and helpful. Some tall order!

If you have never taken part in appraisals before, my intention is to encourage and equip you to do so. If you already have some experience with appraisals, then my aim is to help you make them even better in future. I do hope you find The Perfect Appraisal is right for you. It is, after all, about you. About you doing the right thing, in the right way, at the right time, in the right place, for the right reasons, with the right person. Something you are no doubt trying to achieve in all your working relationships.

Do let me know what you make of The Perfect Appraisal and if you would like further help in making it happen.

Howard Hudson
Training Consultant
'Woodland View'
Churchfields
Stonesfield
Witney
Oxon. OX8 8PP
England   May 1992

Acknowledgements

I am grateful to all those of you who, over the years, have helped my understanding of appraisal. I confess that, in many cases, I cannot recall from whom I have learnt precisely what. My apologies to you, particularly if I have now come to think of your ideas as my own!

However, I do remember where I got some of my ideas. So special thanks to Ted Johns, Terry Morgan and Neil Rackham for your invaluable contributions to my thinking. I am also indebted to Rosemary Tucker and her colleagues at OXFAM for kind permission to use the 'Annual Joint Review' material.

Many thanks to Elizabeth Hennessy my editor – for giving me the opportunity to write this book, and my collaborators Paula Jacobs and Sean Marriott – for helping me put what I wanted to write in a way people want to read.

CHAPTER 1

Appraising Appraisal

– on why it needs to be perfect from start to finish

There's so much good in the worst of us
And so much bad in the best of us,
That it doesn't do for any of us
To sit and judge the rest of us

'It's time for your annual appraisal interview' – words that strike dread into the hearts of many workers each year. Why has appraisal got such a bad reputation, become such a dirty word? Well, what can you expect of a word that the dictionary defines as to do with 'putting a price on, or estimating the value of, something' when it is applied literally to people.

Some people count themselves lucky, for they do not get appraised at all. Others are luckier still, for they get appraised well. The annual appraisal interview does not have to be annual, does not have to be an interview, and certainly does not have to be an 'appraisal' as already defined. The Perfect Appraisal is about 'people frequently meeting to discuss how things are going at work and how they could go even better in future'.

Don't call it 'appraisal'
DO FIND WORDS THAT DO IT JUSTICE

The word 'appraisal' is used in this book as convenient shorthand to refer to the process that you will be trying to make perfect. For many staff, however, the word itself can have negative connotations – is it not, after all, an assessment of their performance? They may feel vulnerable and defensive at the idea that someone (you) will be passing judgement on them. In order to avoid this misconception it may be helpful to describe the process in a way which more accurately suggests its purpose. For instance:

- Performance Improvement and Development
- Progress and Planning
- Joint Review and Action Planning
- Investing in People

Whichever description you use should reflect your approach to the exercise and, as important, should be couched in such terms as will be both acceptable and helpful to those who you will be appraising. The Perfect Appraisal should be seen to be what it is: positive rather than negative; constructive rather than destructive; and forward- rather than backward-looking.

Don't think of it as an 'interview'
DO TREAT IT AS A 'DISCUSSION'

The word 'interview' could bring back painful memories of arduous selection interviews or being hauled over the coals at disciplinary interviews. The key here is to establish the collaborative nature of the appraisal process. In fact, it is not an interview but a discussion – a dialogue

2

in which both parties are involved.

Don't just do it annually
DO IT MUCH MORE FREQUENTLY

Bearing in mind the number of work-related events that occur annually and require your attention as a manager (everything from pay reviews to organizing Christmas parties) it is easy to assume that appraisal is just another chore that needs to be done once every year. Rather, it should be an ongoing process. Even with staff who you feel require little supervision and guidance, who may need no more than one comprehensive appraisal of their 'world of work' per year, you will need regular, and frequent, 'mini' appraisals that look at:

- How the job is going
- How they are doing
- How they can develop
- What you can do to make it happen

The approach to The Perfect Appraisal advocated in this book is equally relevant to both 'mini' appraisals and full appraisals.

Don't include it with salary or disciplinary matters
DO HANDLE THESE THINGS ENTIRELY
SEPARATELY

To introduce such issues at the appraisal will completely destroy its credibility as a 'helping' rather than 'judging' process. It is naive to assume that staff will be prepared to discuss their performance, and its shortcomings, in an open and objective way when they feel that their financial rewards are at stake.

3

Pay reviews and appraisals should be kept several months apart, so that staff can satisfy themselves that the two are not directly linked. Similarly, where merit payments or performance-related bonuses are available, the staff member will have both the incentive and opportunity to act on the results of the appraisal.

Disciplinary issues, in any event, will need to follow a different set of procedures to appraisals. Where such disciplinary procedures are already in motion it will be as well to defer the appraisal until their outcome is clear.

Don't let other people get the wrong impression
DO STRESS AT THE OUTSET WHAT IT IS ALL ABOUT

It is most important that everyone approaches appraisal in a positive frame of mind, or at least with an open mind. Care should be taken to present the process as a means of:

- Learning from the past, as an aid to the future
- Recognizing abilities and potential
- Developing knowledge, skills and attitudes
- Building on successes and overcoming difficulties
- Increasing motivation and job satisfaction
- Enhancing relationships and fostering teamwork

Don't play it by ear
DO PLAN THOROUGHLY

Effective preparation has a vital role to play in the success of any business meeting, and this is particularly true of The Perfect Appraisal. A manifestly ill-prepared manager is sending a quite negative signal to the subject of the appraisal. The inference is that the staff member involved is unworthy of more than cursory individual consideration. Quite aside from this demotivating aspect is the obvious inequity of one, albeit senior, member of staff who has not done his or her job properly coming to discuss the apparent shortcomings of another.

Nevertheless, thorough preparation certainly does not mean setting up a formal and elaborate 'Appraisal System', as this rather mannered approach will merely contribute to misgivings and apprehension about the process. Rather, it is the addressing of the following basic questions in readiness for a 'meeting of minds': Why? Who? Where? When? What? and How? Each of these will be dealt with in great detail over the following chapters.

Don't be the only one to plan
DO ENCOURAGE EVERYONE INVOLVED TO GIVE IT ADVANCE THOUGHT

Preparation is important on both sides, and encouraging staff members' involvement in this way will increase their motivation and sense of 'ownership' of their work. The Perfect Appraisal should be a collaborative venture between management and staff – remember, one-sided planning leads to one-sided discussion and, eventually, one-sided outcomes.

Don't shy away from The Perfect Appraisal
DO TRY IT OUT

Managers and staff alike do tend to fight shy of appraisal; little wonder, given the sensitivities involved and the careful thought needed to handle them sensitively. The Perfect Appraisal, however, can be one of the most rewarding experiences of working life for managers, their staff and the organizations in which they work. It is about enabling people to give of their very best to their work and get the very best from it. So do give it a try once you have read the remaining Do's and Don'ts.

CHAPTER 2

Why Appraise

– on setting objectives for each and every occasion

If you do not know where you are going
How will you know when you have arrived?

By now you should have some feel for why The Perfect Appraisal is not merely desirable, but essential. Managers owe it to their staff, their employers and themselves to engage in regular, thorough and honest appraisals of what can be learnt from the past – as a means of creating a better future.

Don't lose sight of the overall objective
DO HANG ON TO THE FACT THAT IT IS
ABOUT LEARNING AND IMPROVEMENT

It has been established that the overall objective of appraisal is to learn from the past so as to improve in future – but is that really an objective? Future improvement of what exactly? Perhaps it could be improvement in terms of your staff:

- Having a more complete and accurate picture of their present abilities and future potential
- Gaining greater knowledge, developing better skills and holding more positive attitudes
- Experiencing more successes and fewer difficulties with work
- Feeling more motivated and satisfied with work
- Enjoying more rewarding working relationships and a greater sense of co-operative teamwork

Don't set generalized, vague and 'woolly' objectives
DO BE VERY SPECIFIC

As appealing as the above statements may be, acknowledging them as objectives will provide little constructive aid in clearly identifying and attaining your overall objective. You need to look behind the words to establish how you will encourage them to 'Feel more motivated . . .', 'Gain greater knowledge . . .' and so on.

Don't set objectives about your inputs
DO ALWAYS THINK IN TERMS OF THEIR OUTPUTS

Another common problem with these statements is that they all relate to what is being invested in people (your inputs) rather than what they will produce from people (their outputs). The Perfect Appraisal is all about enabling people to give of their very best at work as well as getting the very best from it. Ultimately, you must ensure that the fact that staff members have these things (greater knowledge, increased motivation etc.) will result in real improvements in their performance.

Don't assume that certain areas of performance cannot be measured
DO TRY TO SET MEASURABLE STANDARDS FOR EVERYTHING

In order to identify and acknowledge areas for improved performance you must first establish the basis on which this is to be assessed – how will you recognize it when you see it? There are a number of abstract aspects to staff performance which are, in themselves, impossible to quantify precisely. What can be assessed, however, is the end result – the effect that these intangible aspects have on their output. In this way it is possible to turn a **qualitative** aspect of someone's performance into something **quantitative**, that can then be measured.

Don't set the same objectives for everyone
DO SELECT THE MOST APPROPRIATE ONES FOR EACH PERSON

Although this may seem obvious, it is quite often the case that managers will set common objectives, with common standards of performance, for all their staff. This is, presumably, on the basis that they are all doing the same job and can therefore be expected to perform at identical levels – by inference it would be unfair to do anything other than treat them all the same.

Although the overall objective – improved performance – is the same, the means by which each individual will achieve this is likely to be quite different. This involves taking account of your staff's different abilities and stages of development, then responding to each individual accordingly. In other words, you must **treat everyone differently in order to treat them equally**.

For each and every appraisal that you conduct, you will need to ask yourself: 'What specifically should I be aiming to achieve with this person, at this time?' You should then set your objectives based on:

- Key areas of their work (which may or may not be the same as for other employees)
- Their track record of performance
- Your previous discussions with them (if there have been any) about standards and performance, also their reactions to such discussions

Don't give equal priority to all your objectives
DO RANK THEM IN ORDER OF IMPORTANCE

It is tempting to expect people to improve unilaterally on all the key areas of their work where there is scope for significant development: 'It is all important!' is the understandable reaction of many managers. Nevertheless, some things – if you are honest with yourself – will inevitably be more important than others. You should therefore prioritize your objectives:

- **Must** be achieved – those which you feel you must get accepted as they are vital to the job, or those where current performance is particularly weak.
- **Should** be achieved – those which you feel should be aimed for, but which could be tackled at a later date should this appraisal prove difficult
- **Could** be achieved – those which are not crucial to your vision of a better future but which may be raised if the appraisal goes particularly well

Even with the top priority objectives you will notice the wording is '. . . which you **feel** you must get accepted'.

10

This serves as a reminder of the most important factor in setting objectives for The Perfect Appraisal – a workable degree of flexibility.

Don't be inflexible in your approach
DO BE OPEN-MINDED ABOUT WHAT YOU MIGHT ACHIEVE

Although you have prioritized your objectives, you may have to accept that you will need to leave a degree of latitude as to how quickly and comprehensively they are likely to be achieved. This may go against the grain for many managers will feel that, ultimately, they have the right to impose their expectations and objectives upon their staff. How much better it will be, though, if your staff willingly accept those objectives as ones that they can realistically achieve.

You must set your staff challenges, but not ones that they feel are beyond their reach as this could defeat them before they even begin. Using the 'small steps' approach you may lead your staff on to achieving far more substantial overall objectives via a series of small progressions over a period of time.

Don't put all the onus on other people to change their ways
DO THINK HOW YOU CAN HELP THINGS ALONG

It is worth remembering that when you set objectives for others you are also, effectively, setting them for yourself – a sobering thought. You must take the time to assess exactly what it is that you require from a staff member and the manner in which you can accurately measure their performance. The Perfect Appraisal requires you to understand and take into account the needs and motivations of your staff. For instance:

- Acknowledge that the staff member may have hitherto been aware of the importance of the issue that you have now brought to their attention – you are therefore not criticizing them, merely highlighting the need for something to be done.
- Allow a reasonable amount of time for the improvement to occur – setting a realistic target date
- Offer any additional help that may be needed – resources, guidance, training etc.
- Agree to reduce their workload – so that they may concentrate on making the improvement
- Be prepared to concede, even, that you may not have previously made your expectations clear – when you specified required standards of performance

**Don't set objectives which people will resent
DO CHOOSE THINGS THAT THEY WILL FEEL
COMMITTED TO ACHIEVING**

Most people will agree that they are not perfect – we can all improve. Nevertheless, should you highlight a particular area for improvement in someone's work, their first reaction will instinctively be one of resentment at this implied criticism. Their second reaction will be to question it:

- 'Where is your evidence that I need to improve?'
- 'What level of improvement do you have in mind?'
- 'By when am I expected to make this improvement, given all the other things I have on at the moment?'

In order to make your objective one that a staff member

can feel more committed on doing something about, you will need to:

- Convince them as to why it is so important – not only to you, but to the organization and, more importantly, to them
- Explain precisely what your expectations are – the standards of performance you require
- Be specific in your appraisal of how far, and in what way, their performance currently falls short of the required standard
- Give a realistic timeframe in which all this improvement can occur

As to overcoming that first reaction – one of resentment – it is worth accepting the premise that, for the recipient at least, there is no such thing as constructive criticism, however carefully it is put. You may, therefore, have to accept some initial resentment and turn the other cheek to it. Nevertheless, this is no excuse not to put your criticism as carefully as possible – a point we shall return to at length when we look at how to appraise.

CHAPTER 3

Who Appraise

– on involving all concerned in the process

Who am I and who are you?
If that we knew the answer to,
If I knew you and you knew me,
A better place the world would be!

The preceding chapters have already stressed the collaborative nature of appraisal. Now would be a good point at which to turn your thoughts to all the other people involved in the appraisal process and ask: '**Who** should be involved and **how** should they be involved?'

Don't select some of your staff to be appraised, and exclude others
DO OFFER APPRAISALS TO EVERYONE

Some managers only appraise those staff who they see as poor performers – presumably on the basis that problems must be dealt with, whereas things that are going well can be left alone. This approach gives rise to complaints from those called in that they are being discriminated against, and gives appraisal a bad name – making it seem more like disciplining. On the other hand, those who are not appraised can feel they are being neglected – even though you trust them, they still need some of our time occasionally.

You may alternatively find yourself avoiding appraisals of staff with whom you have a problem, only appraising those to whom you can easily relate.

Suspicion and misconception will result from appraising some staff and not others – the answer is to offer appraisals to everyone. Not all staff will relish the prospect at first, but they will at least be reassured by seeing that everyone is in the same position.

Don't tackle the 'toughest nuts' first
DO START WITH THOSE WHO ARE WILLING AND ABLE

Build up your confidence in using appraisal skills in relatively straightforward situations before trying them out in more challenging ones. This way the appraisals you conduct will get a good reputation – people will be keen to join in. With those people who remain negative, or apathetic, it is worth explaining that you are using a new approach which can be jointly reviewed afterwards.

Don't plan things simply from your point of view
DO ALSO CONSIDER HOW OTHERS SEE THINGS

You know how you view the person you are appraising, but it is also useful to think how others – their colleagues/other managers/your superiors – view them. If you are new to the job you will, in any event, need to consult with your superior and any other managers for whom your staff member does work.

This approach will also enable you to look at their

performance in different areas of the job. You may discover that they are not, by nature, lazy/obstructive/demotivated etc. but merely adopt these characteristics when dealing with certain aspects of their work or, indeed, certain other members of staff.

You must also, of course, take into account the staff member's likely reactions and objections to the points you need to raise with them. In this way you can pre-empt possible areas of conflict or sticking points within the appraisal.

Don't just do your own homework
DO ENCOURAGE THEM TO DO THEIRS TOO

Several other points have stressed the need for a collaborative approach (one-sided planning leads to one-sided outcomes) and by involving your staff members in the preparation for their appraisal you are helping to establish this. Having been given the opportunity to assess themselves, they will feel greater involvement and will be far more likely to view the appraisal positively (as a discussion), rather than negatively (the 'school report' syndrome).

The Annual Joint Review form featured in Appendix 1 illustrates a useful approach. Each party is asked the same questions in preparation for the appraisal, thus ensuring that they have both given consideration to the same issues.

Don't only think about action the two of you can take
DO INCLUDE OTHER PEOPLE IN YOUR PLANS

The Perfect Appraisal should not be carried out in a vacuum. In discussing your mutual needs and objectives, pay close attention to the implications these have for the members of staff working alongside, above, or below the appraisee. How, for example, might they play a part in helping them achieve their objectives?

You should also consult with your Personnel and Training Department in advance, to check what is available to help with whatever training needs or career development opportunities you may have in mind for your staff member.

Don't feel you have to appraise everyone yourself
DO DELEGATE THINGS WHEREVER YOU CAN

Within your sphere of responsibility you may well have more members of staff than you could effectively appraise. Particularly where one or more links in the command chain separate you from a member of staff, feel free to delegate the task to one of your immediate subordinates – and remember when you come to appraise them that it is your responsibility to set an appropriate example of how to conduct The Perfect Appraisal!

Quite aside from the practical necessity to delegate is the desirability of having members of staff appraised by the managers to whom they are most closely linked.

Don't wait for others to start the process
DO YOUR OWN THING ONCE YOU ARE READY

Merely because your manager has not seen fit to take the lead in organizing his or her own staff appraisals, do not feel that this should inhibit you as you set about appraising your staff. In fact, should you do so you will be in a position of far greater authority when your manager eventually comes to assess you. A system of appraisals that works from the bottom up tends to leave people at every level much better prepared to approach their own appraisal.

Similarly, if other departments have made no moves in this direction, don't wait for them. Nevertheless, you may need to pre-empt your own staff's objections ('If they aren't doing it why do we have to bother . . .') by emphasizing its benefits to them.

CHAPTER 4

Where Appraise

– on choosing the right location and layout

A place for everything,
And everything in its place

The environment in which you hold your discussion can make or break The Perfect Appraisal. It is most important, therefore, that you give careful consideration to finding the right setting and, having found it, that you set it up correctly.

Don't allow any interruptions
DO GET AWAY FROM IT ALL

This is a crucial aspect of conducting The Perfect Appraisal. Quite aside from the dangers of losing the thread of your discussing, allowing yourself to be interrupted will also give the staff member a pretty negative impression of the importance you have placed on their appraisal. If they do not feel that you have made it a priority, you cannot expect them to commit themselves to it wholeheartedly.

If you are holding the appraisal in your own office it

is vital that you are not interrupted. Both parties must be free to concentrate totally on the discussion. If you are, by nature, a very 'hands on' manager you may need to protect yourself from yourself in the following ways:

- Don't try to do anything else while appraising, don't keep going out to check on other areas of work or other staff – concentrate exclusively on the appraisal
- Ask somebody else (a 'gatekeeper') to deal with telephone calls and visitors – don't attempt to do it yourself
- Warn your other staff in advance that you will not be available – it is only fair to give them adequate notice
- Put a notice on the door to indicate a meeting is in progress

Don't automatically choose 'home' or 'away' venues
DO CONSIDER FINDING NEUTRAL GROUND

Your office is not necessarily the best place to conduct an appraisal. Apart from the ever-present risk of interruptions, it can be intimidating for the appraisee, particularly if they have been there recently about a disciplinary or grievance matter. The appraisee's office is not always an ideal site either, as your presence there could be misinterpreted by third parties.

Find a neutral place, somewhere that you can both concentrate without feeling you are playing at 'home' or 'away'. The best solution is to book a quiet office at work or, if there really isn't one available, to find a quiet room in a hotel or other public venue. Busy restaurants and cafés are not recommended – you will not be able to talk freely if you feel people are listening to every work, or if you are tackling a plate of spaghetti!

Don't stick to the usual room layout
DO PREPARE THE VENUE TO SUIT APPRAISALS

If you do use an office, particularly if it is your own, avoid the traditional arrangement of furniture, where people face each other across a desk. Experience has shown that 'coming out from behind the desk' (literally and metaphorically) and sitting at right angles to each other, with or without a table, is better. Weighed against the benefits of this, however, you must remember that a change in layout can make people suspicious – and it is imperative that both parties feel as comfortable as possible if you are to achieve a positive outcome to the appraisal.

There are several other steps you can take to prepare the venue effectively:

* Ensure your chair is not higher than the appraisee's chair – if so, they will feel at a disadvantage
* Avoid sitting with your back to the light – the appraisee will be dazzled, confronted by a silhouette and thus feel like the subject of an interrogation
* Lay out the room so that neither party will be facing the window – this can be distracting
* Adjust the temperature of the room if necessary – you are likely to be there for some time

Don't just provide materials for yourself
DO THINK WHAT YOU WILL BOTH NEED

As has been stressed, The Perfect Appraisal is reliant on the active participation of **both** parties involved. This area of your preparation provides another opportunity for you to promote an atmosphere of co-operation and collaboration. For instance, you could:

- Explain why you are taking notes – invite the appraisee to do so too
- Provide the necessary equipment for both of you to make notes – sufficient pens and paper and something to rest them on
- Try using a flipchart – this is ideal for 'brainstorming' (recording and assimilating all the ideas you both have on a particular area)
- Make arrangements for refreshments – as you are going to be there for some time this will keep it from feeling like an endurance test

Don't forget to book things well ahead
DO CHECK OUT FACILITIES IN ADVANCE

You should try to book the room well in advance of the appraisal and confirm where you will be meeting with the appraisee. This will give adequate time to relocate if, for some legitimate reason, the appraisee feels it is unsuitable. Then, on the day of the appraisal make sure to:

- Be there on time, or arrange for the room to be open – you don't want the appraisee waiting outside a locked door until you arrive
- Leave yourself enough time – don't let that last-minute telephone call sabotage all your preparation and cause you to arrive at the meeting both harassed and late
- 'Walk the stage' – do a preliminary check of the meeting room to plan the layout and pre-empt any potential problems; you don't want to have to waste the first ten minutes of the appraisal doing this

CHAPTER 5

When Appraise

– on finding the best time and allowing enough of it

> *There will never be enough time,*
> *But remember –*
> *We all have all the time there is!*

It may be all too infrequently that you can find time to sit down and have a carefully considered conversation with individual members of staff. You must, therefore, make sure that you do just that with their appraisal, and spend a few minutes, at least, considering your skilful use of time and timing.

Don't announce it 'cold' on the day
DO GIVE AT LEAST A WEEK'S ADVANCE NOTICE

This is all part of taking the appraisal seriously and being seen to do so. Quite aside from this being common courtesy, it will also save the appraisee from feeling you are trying to pressurize them. Additionally, you will both need time to prepare yourselves. For instance, to:

- Plan which items you want to raise
- Research information on specific issues

- Reschedule or delegate other work
- Establish and agree an appropriate length for the appraisal

Don't choose a time when you are preoccupied with other things
DO GIVE IT YOUR UNDIVIDED ATTENTION

It cannot be stressed too often that total concentration on your part can make all the difference to the course and outcome of an appraisal. Any distraction can cause you to miss signals the appraisee is sending you. An area in which he or she takes particular pride, and is keen to develop, which is ignored by you, can result in disillusionment and demotivation. The subtle warning signs of an impending power struggle, or personality conflict within the department, can be invaluable to you in averting potential disaster.

So plan the appraisal for a relatively quiet time of the year or month, thereby avoiding month-end/year-end/pre- or post-holiday chaos and crises.

At the appraisal, once the discussion is under way, it is important to capitalize on the time you have got available by devoting your attention to what is being said without feeling constrained by timetables, looking at your watch, or otherwise appearing anxious, will send a negative signal to your staff member – it will be apparent to them that they are not your first priority, and they will be demotivated.

Don't just pick a time that suits you personally
DO CHECK WHEN WILL BE CONVENIENT FOR BOTH OF YOU

Taking into consideration your staff member's workload and schedule will give another clear indication of the collaborative nature of the appraisal. You should also bear in mind that you will have, amongst your workforce, a variety of 'larks' and 'owls'. In other words, there will be those who perform far better first thing in the morning, while they are fresh, and those who are at their best as the day progresses.

Timing is also important where you feel that there are serious issues to be tackled. A Friday afternoon appointment leaves the weekend for people to pause and reflection what has been discussed. On the other hand, a Monday morning appraisal could leave an entire week of misgivings and resentment to build up, without the opportunity for your staff members to distance them-selves from the work environment and regain their objectivity.

Don't postpone it
DO GO THROUGH WITH IT

Having asked your staff member to devote valuable time to preparing for, and participating in, the appraisal, any postponement could be met with resentment. As before, this will send a potentially negative signal as to the value you place on them or their time.

Where a postponement is absolutely unavoidable, you should at least take the time to speak briefly and explain the position you find yourself in, being careful to reiterate the importance of the appraisal to you. Explain that you need to schedule another meeting where you will have long enough to do justice to the issues involved, and arrange a mutually convenient time to reconvene.

It is worth remembering that any postponement of the appraisal will necessarily result in the extension of timescales for subsequent action.

Don't be late
DO GET THERE AHEAD OF TIME

It is particularly easy for a manager who has a 'hands on' approach to be waylaid whilst heading for an appraisal – by a last-minute telephone call, for instance, or an urgent problem on the shopfloor. It is most important, however, for you to arrive slightly ahead of time in order to prepare yourself for the appraisal. No matter how much preparation you have done, arriving late, breathless and apologetic will undoubtedly get things off to a bad start.

Don't try to fit too many into a day
DO A MAXIMUM OF TWO APPRAISALS PER DAY

In order to give of your best at each appraisal, you must pace yourself. However pressured you may feel to give all of your staff personal attention, this will ultimately be counter-productive where you are responsible for large numbers of people. In order to stay 'fresh', limit your workload to preferably one, or at the most two, appraisals a day and, of course, feel free to delegate appraisals wherever possible.

Don't rush it
DO ALLOW PLENTY OF TIME

For full appraisals allow at least two hours, to do justice to your staff member's 'world of work'. Should the appraisal overrun its allotted time, remember that it is always an option to adjourn the appraisal and finish it at a later date. This is preferable to rushing through the agenda in order to feel you have covered everything, but not doing it properly so that it's a waste of time. In the long run, it is more effective to cover some of the topics comprehensively and return to the others later, than to skim over a vast range of issues without satisfactorily resolving any of them.

If you want to adjourn, explain that important issues are being raised, and that in order to do them justice you propose to return to them later when they can be examined more thoroughly. Then fix a mutually convenient time to resume.

Don't allow the same amount of time for everyone
DO THINK HOW LONG INDIVIDUALS ARE LIKELY TO NEED

Rigidly keeping to a timetable which allows an equal amount of time to each appraisal may superficially appear to be the most equitable arrangement. It is more effective, however, to treat people fairly by treating them differently – tailoring the time you spend to their individual needs. The time needed will vary between:

- Different staff members
- The same staff member over time

The first time you appraise someone who is new, or who has recently been transferred to your staff from elsewhere, you will obviously need to cover far more ground than you will with a person you have been appraising for several years. The paramount consideration here is the establishment of a good relationship between the two of you, as time invested in this will reap substantial dividends later on.

A person whose appraisal would be quite straightforward under normal circumstances, but who is temporarily facing stress at work, will need more attention, and consequently a longer appraisal, at such times than they otherwise would.

In such cases as these, full appraisals could take at least half a day.

Don't appraise everyone with the same frequency
DO AGREE APPROPRIATE INTERVALS WITH EACH PERSON

The precise frequency with which you need to appraise your staff will depend on how complex their jobs are and how capable they are.

Everyone should receive a comprehensive appraisal at least annually to take stock of 'where they are, where they are going, and how they get there'. This will probably suffice for staff who hold straightforward jobs in which they are very experienced.

However, a new recruit to the organization or someone who has recently been promoted and is taking on new responsibilities may need to be appraised at monthly or even weekly intervals initially. Careful monitoring in this way can avert potential problems before they arise and build up the staff member's abilities in the new sphere. It will also develop his or her confidence in the appraisal process.

When people are transferred, promoted or faced by unexpected upheaval in their workplace, frequent appraisal can be very effective in helping them to survive the transition.

Similarly, with established members of staff whose work is fairly complex you should consider arranging 'mini' appraisals of work progress and plans, to occur at least every six months, and preferably quarterly. In this way, both of you can keep your fingers on the overall 'pulse'. These 'mini' appraisals should be approached in just the same way as full appraisals, although they will obviously not take as long to prepare for or conduct.

So do agree appropriate intervals for appraisal with everyone individually.

Don't leave everything until the last minute
DO IT WELL IN ADVANCE

A final reminder that, having allowed yourself plenty of time to prepare things thoroughly, you must use that time wisely. You have quite probably experienced events which have turned out to be non-events through inadequate last-minute preparations. This is never more true than of the inadequately-prepared appraisal.

CHAPTER 6

What Appraise

– on deciding what ground to cover, and not to cover

Give me the courage to change the things I can,
The grace to accept the things I can't
And the wisdom to know the difference

You will now see precisely why you need to give so much time to The Perfect Appraisal. This is where we get down to considering the detailed content of your forthcoming discussion with your staff member. It will be a wide-ranging and quite complex agenda you need to consider, covering many aspects of his or her past, present and future working life. This chapter suggests what – and what not – to cover, also in what sequence to cover it.

Don't simply appraise their work
DO COVER THEIR WHOLE 'WORLD OF WORK'

You should try to establish an agenda that not only reflects how they perform their given tasks, but also covers their working relationships and career aspirations. (See the example at Appendix 1.) Find out who they work with and what quality of support they provide or feel they receive. Establish how they see their future and what their aspirations are in terms of career development.

Don't talk in terms of tasks
DO TALK ABOUT RESPONSIBILITIES AND PERFORMANCE

When you establish targets you must always think in terms of an end result, as opposed to the possible means by which this may be achieved. In other words – don't give people tasks, give them responsibility. In this way you can pre-empt any temptation to impose your own views on how your staff members' targets should be achieved. They, in turn, will feel more involved and more motivated to achieve the results you require.
Equally, when you come to appraise their progress, you do not need to look at what tasks they have completed – rather look at what they have made of them and assess how they could make even more of them. Between you, try to identify what aspects have been particularly successful and discuss how the appraisee sees their job developing.

Don't over-emphasize extremes of performance
DO CONCENTRATE MORE ON AVERAGE PERFORMANCE

Your objective should be to encourage your staff to develop. Many managers make the mistake of concentrating on the 'peaks and troughs' in their staff's performance. What will prove more useful, however, is to look at things which are currently all right – possibly representing the major part of your staff member's work – and focusing on ways of making them better.

Traditionally, up to three-quarters of the time in appraisals is spent concentrating on negative aspects of performance. By contrast, The Perfect Appraisal uses three-quarters of the time to focus on areas of average to high performance, areas which are good and which could be even better.

The 'Perfect' approach will ensure that you don't make the mistake of seeing people with 'halo or horns' – as all good or all bad.

Don't be an archaeologist
DO BE A FORTUNE TELLER

Another common failing amongst managers is to spend the majority of the appraisal looking at present and past performance. They may spend up to 90 per cent of the appraisal discussing this, relegating the future to a measly 10 per cent of the available discussion.

Although important lessons can be learnt from past successes and failures, the most positive results will be obtained by using these as a launchpad to discussing future performance. In fact, a good half of The Perfect Appraisal should be devoted to focusing on the future. A major aspect of your preparation should, therefore, be to draft plans of action relating to both the appraisee's short- and long-term development.

Don't make promises you can't keep
DO LAY PLANS YOU CAN FOLLOW THROUGH

However much enthusiasm may be generated at the time of the appraisal, with regard to future plans, do be realistic as to what can be achieved and what you are able to contribute to this. You should not raise staff expectations unless you are confident that you can fulfil them. It is far better to promise less but consistently follow through – your staff will respect your input far more as a result.

Equally, don't back yourself into a corner by issuing threats beyond your authority, or indeed **any** threats at all. Look for constructive ways of dealing with any problems that fall within your scope of authority.

Don't simply concentrate on your agenda
DO ANTICIPATE THEIRS AS WELL

You should always try to tap into the appraisees' areas of interest – their motivations and aspirations – accepting that their priorities for discussion may be different to your own. Also take into account their working environment – other people and other factors that have a significant influence on the appraisee and his or her performance.

So, when you prepare for the appraisal, ask yourself what issues they may raise – for instance, what mitigating circumstances they may cite, with regard to their performance, and what other people they may try to involve. Remember, you have actively encouraged them to be prepared to talk about their 'world of work' as **they** see it.

Don't be caught on the hop
DO EXPECT THE UNEXPECTED

Do your homework, accepting that however much you take into account prior to the appraisal, issues will still arise for which you are totally unprepared. Where their priorities are wildly different from your own, as painstakingly laid out in your agenda, be prepared to take a whole new approach at a moment's notice. As we have said – expect the unexpected.

Good preparation is really about looking at what **might** happen, rather than planning what **will** happen.

Don't just think about improving their performance
DO ACKNOWLEDGE THAT YOU COULD ALSO IMPROVE YOURS

This aspect of appraisal seems to be a sticking point for many managers who fall into the trap of implying: 'We're not here to talk about **me** – we're here to talk about **you** and how **you** need to pull your socks up!'

In reality, it is most important for you to ask the appraisees how they feel about that part of **your** job that directly affects them. Consider what **you** can do to improve your working relationship, and help them to increase their performance. Ask: 'What more can I do for you as your manager?' You may feel you are risking a response like 'Well, get off my back for a start . . .' or 'Give me a company car . . .' when in fact the response is far more likely to match the offer, and be positive.

Where this approach **does** yield criticism of some kind, remember not to feel defensive. Plan to deal with it, as you would expect the appraisee to, in the collaborative spirit of the appraisal.

Don't get involved appraising other people
DO FOCUS ON THE PAIR OF YOU

It is difficult not to let the performance or attitude of other staff members be brought into the discussion. They are, after all, part of the appraisee's world of work.

What you should avoid, however, is being drawn into commenting on these other staff members – it is, after all, not **their** appraisal!

What you must do is narrow the agenda. So, having let them talk about their colleagues – plan to bring things back as soon as possible to the topics that are directly relevant to **your** working relationship.

Don't be a butterfly
DO BE A BEE

Having decided what topics should be on the agenda, the next step is to establish in what order to take them. Rather than 'butterflying' from one subject to another at random, the appraisal should ideally make a 'beeline' for topics one at a time, settle on them until they are completed, then move on – following a nice smooth path from start to finish.

Appendix 1 provides a useful example of how to do this with all your staff. It divides the agenda into five separate sections to be taken in turn. Individually and collectively, these sections also follow the logic of leading on from the past and present into the future. This will provide you with a flexible template which allows you to switch topics without losing the central thread.

Don't plan to follow the plan slavishly
DO MAKE IT WORK BEST FOR BOTH OF YOU

As with so many aspects of appraisal, you must remain flexible. Always try to start on a positive – i.e. areas of strength which will, of course, vary for each individual. You can therefore have no hard and fast rules on which precise area (attitude, technical skills or whatever) to start the appraisal.

Equally, if the appraisee raises an issue before you had planned to, try to weave it into the discussion rather than saying: 'I'm coming to that in a minute!' Remember that appraisal is a conversation not a monologue.

CHAPTER 7

How Appraise

– on conducting the conversation in the most productive way

> *If I lead you may not follow*
> *If I follow you may not lead*
> *So please just walk beside me*

Once the preparation is complete, you can get on with the appraisal discussing. Well, not quite, for you need to plan the conversation even more carefully than you have prepared everything else. It's not what you say, it's the way that you say it – that's what counts.

Don't get carried away with your own enthusiasm
DO ALLOW FOR THEIR ENTHUSIASM TOO

The more planning you do before an appraisal, the more ideas you are likely to have in mind for your staff member. Too many appraisals go wrong because, albeit with the best of intentions, managers overwhelm the appraisee with their own enthusiasm for the exciting vision of the future that they have created in their plans.

Guard against this by giving your appraisee opportunities to be enthusiastic too.

Don't talk too much
DO GIVE THE OTHER PERSON EQUAL OPPORTUNITY TO SPEAK

Appraisal consists of a joint discussion leading to jointly-agreed action. Both parties should therefore enjoy an equal share of the time to have their say.

Some people will readily take their opportunity to have an equal say. Others, however, will need plenty of encouragement to give their views – either because they expect you to take the lead or they are nervous, wary even, about what is to come.

The art of The Perfect Appraisal discussion is applying the skills that come naturally with those you find it easy to get on with, when dealing with those you don't. You must give everyone a fair chance to express their views fully from the moment that the appraisal starts.

Don't get straight down to business
DO SPEND A BIT OF TIME WARMING UP FIRST

There is a temptation to want to get down to business straight away. Resist it. It is the first of four traps of over-enthusiasm.

Time spent in introduction is very important to establish rapport, to get both parties to the appraisal warmed up for a productive discussion. First set the tone of the conversation, emphasizing the value of joint discussion, then set the scene, outlining the purpose and structure of the appraisal.

Don't go on too long with your introduction
DO GET THEM TALKING VERY EARLY ON

Having set the scene from your point of view, you

should pause and ask how they see it, continuing the discussion once you are satisfied. The second of the four traps of over-enthusiasm awaits you here – having established rapport effectively you can destroy it all too easily with a few ill-chosen words that, even if not intended to do so, sound like: 'Right, that's the formalities over, now let's get on with it.'

Don't switch rapport on and off like a tap
DO KEEP IT RUNNING THROUGHOUT THE CONVERSATION

If you use rapport only for the warm-up, appraisees will think you are just going through the motions of limbering up, or softening them up, for the real contest – and immediately become suspicious. Remember, you need them on your side.

Don't lead off by giving your views
DO INVITE APPRAISEES TO GIVE THEIRS FIRST

Trap three of over-enthusiasm, having established rapport, is to launch into your own review of the past and vision of the future. A golden rule for handing all stages of The Perfect Appraisal is to encourage the appraisee to give his or her views before you give yours.

This is the most effective way of ensuring a genuinely joint discussion which leads to genuine jointly-agreed action. If your staff members can see early on in the conversation that their views really count – by being encouraged to put them first as the basis of subsequent discussion – then the majority of their fears and reservations about appraisal will disappear at a stroke.

This is particularly important when discussing ways in which their performance could improve in future.

These are issues about which your staff members can easily get defensive if you raise them – it's much better for them to be given a chance to identify their own short-comings and ideas for improvement, which they may well do if asked the right questions.

Don't ask closed or leading questions
DO USE PLENTY OF OPEN-ENDED ONES

Open questions encourage others to speak freely, to make thorough and honest self-assessments, and to lay the foundations for future action. For example:

- Why do you think this has proved difficult?
- Who could give you help with that?
- Where is the best place to try it out?
- When would be a good time to start?
- What can you do to help things along?
- How will you go about it?

Closed or leading questions, on the other hand, often literally close down the options for reply – they may even try to lead the appraisee to a specific response. Questions like these can, in fact, simply be answered 'Yes' or 'No', if a person so chooses. They may be necessary for ascertaining specific details as the appraisal develops, but do not promote joint discussion or, indeed, tell you whether you have really obtained joint commitment.

So, avoid phrasing questions in a close/leading way which would mean, taking the examples above:

- Do/Don't you think this has proved difficult because . . . ?
- Could/couldn't you get help with that from . . . ?

- Is/isn't the best place to try it out . . . ?
- Would/wouldn't a good time to start be . . . ?
- Can/can't you help things along by . . . ?
- Will/won't you go about it by . . . ?

Don't start by asking difficult and sensitive questions
DO GET THEM TALKING BEFORE YOU GET
THEM THINKING

In the same way as the introduction 'warms up' the whole discussion, it is also advisable to warm up on each topic covered. Appendix 1 demonstrates how to put questions into a helpful sequence to aid the flow of the discussion. For instance, under 'The Job', the first questions concern what both parties see as the staff member's main tasks and responsibilities – something which they should be able to discuss fairly freely, even if they don't see them in exactly the same way. Next, they look at the more sensitive topic of performance in these areas – considering things that have gone well before things that have proved difficult. Finally, they talk about possible developments, in terms of improvements or changes for the future.

The same pattern is repeated for other topics, building up to a jointly-agreed action plan. More comprehensive checklists of questions useful for Reviewing and Improving Performance are given at Appendices 2 and 3. These follow the recommended pattern of starting with general questions, then more specific and, finally, probing ones.

Don't ask too many questions
DO TAKE ONE THING AT A TIME

Trap four of over-enthusiasm consists of getting carried

away by asking questions. If there are too many, the meeting will feel like an interrogation to the person on the receiving end. Questions should therefore be limited to those which enable you to do your job thoroughly **and** which will appear relevant and helpful to the appraisee.

Equally, if they all come at once this will be very confusing:

'Which aspects of your job do you particularly like or dislike, and which do you find most challenging!'

This will not only confuse the appraisee, but will also give them the opportunity to pick out the question they want to answer and leave the others unresolved.

Don't be afraid of silence
DO ALLOW TIME TO THINK

Resist the temptation to follow up a question too quickly when it does not get an instant reply. Your questions are designed to stimulate thought and, however well prepared the appraisee may be, they will need time to collect their thoughts, refer to their notes and plan their response.

Don't interrupt their thinking time – having asked them a question, mentally count to ten before saying anything else (while keeping an eye on them, to check they are not too baffled, incensed or upset by your question to answer it). You also need time to think, of course, and can use this pause to consider where their answer might take things next.

Don't forget to listen carefully to their answers
DO GIVE THEM YOUR FULL ATTENTION

You must pay just as much attention to the answers you are getting as to the questions you ask. To help you do this, and to help the other person see that you are doing it, listen actively.

For instance, employ what could be called the 'Look, Nod, Grunt and Smile Routine':

- Don't look up at the ceiling – congratulating yourself on the question you have just asked
- Don't look out of the window – admiring the world passing by
- Don't look down at your notes – half planning what to do next
- Do look at the other person – literally reading their lips, thereby taking in far more than you can with your ears alone
- Do nod – not nod off!
- Do grunt – 'Uh, huh . . . I see . . . mmm . . . really?'
- Do smile – where appropriate!

All of this indicates that you are interested in and closely following what is being said – not that you necessarily agree with it (more on that shortly).

Don't assume anything
DO CHECK IT OUT

However hard you concentrate you won't be able to register 100 per cent of what the other person says. Even if you think you have grasped the main points, can you be absolutely sure? It can be very dangerous to make assumptions.

The appraisee may make several points in the same breath as a response to an open-ended question. The reply may seem disjointed, rambling or ambiguous. In such cases it is imperative to check that you have understood precisely what is being said before commenting on it or, indeed, ignoring it because you have found it confusing:

- 'Let me make sure I have got all your points on this, they are . . . is that right?'
- 'So the main thing you feel is . . . is it?'
- 'When you say . . . does it mean you think . . . ?'

It would be pedantic to do this after every response to every question, but you should certainly check your understanding following each batch of questions and answers on a specific topic – particularly as things may not occur in the nice neat order that you had planned.

Don't press on regardless with your plan
DO RESPOND TO THEIR RESPONSES

You will often get responses to your questions that do not lead you naturally to the next thing you had intended to raise. This is the nature of dynamic discussions, and the art of conducting them is to have a plan to refer to – making sure the necessary points are covered – but to use it flexibly.

As a general rule you should go with the flow wherever possible, talking about issues as and when the appraisee raises them, rather than when you had planned to raise them. These issues are obviously uppermost in their mind. They will appreciate it, therefore, if you follow them up there and then, and will be disappointed if you don't. They may not even be able to concentrate on what you want to raise next unless you have cleared their mind of their concerns first.

Don't be drawn into giving your views too soon
DO PERSIST WITH ASKING BEFORE TELLING

Resist the temptation to comment too early on what the appraisee says. This can happen all too easily, especially when they have said something that you were not expecting. Do persist with asking them questions to explore their views thoroughly before responding. This participative approach is most important because it will allow them to take ownership of the topics and solutions discussed. They are therefore more likely to act upon decisions made during the appraisal and are less likely to react defensively when tackling difficult issues.

In order to keep the appraisee talking, it is perfectly legitimate for you to answer their questions with questions of your own, clarifying their position before committing yourself to passing comment.

Having asked all your questions on a particular topic, and listened carefully to the answers, you will then, of course, need to make some sort of response to what your staff member has been saying.

Consider the manager who had spent all the appraisal skilfully questioning and listening in a way which enabled the staff member to work out a superb action plan for himself – just like the one the manager would have suggested anyway. As they were leaving, however, the manager noticed that the appraisee looked rather disappointed, so asked yet another question: 'What's up? Aren't you happy with what we've achieved?' 'Yes,' came the reply, 'but I would still like to know what you think of me!'

Don't let opportunities to be supportive slip by
DO EXPRESS APPROVAL WHENEVER YOU CAN

When responding, always remember to say when you like something that your staff member has said or done: 'I agree . . .'; 'That's a very good point . . .'; 'You made a really good job of that . . .'.

Managers often hold back from offering praise because of:

- Embarrassment at paying compliments
- Fear that it will be encouraging someone to 'rest on their laurels'
- Belief that it is unnecessary – 'silence implies consent' or even 'they are only doing what is expected of them, and what they are paid for'
- Apprehension that staff will be suspicious of their motives – wary of management merely going through the motions, softening them up or even fishing for compliments in return

You should overcome any such feelings because being supportive is a crucial ingredient in reinforcing the spirit of co-operation that is at the very heart of The Perfect Appraisal.

Don't float your ideas in the air
DO BUILD THEM ON SOLID GROUND

In order to establish a workable action plan with the appraisees, you will need to ask them plenty of questions about their ideas for the future. This will enable you to identify or create areas of common ground on which to build. The emphasis should be on fostering mutual aims and goals – collaboration before negotiation.

If your staff members feel they are being given a fair hearing they are more likely to be co-operative and receptive to your suggestions. When listening to their ideas, think how they tie in with what you want to see happen, and whether you can now build in any similar points of your own. Furthermore, when putting forward your ideas, highlight your common aims. Do not use 'Yes, but . . .', use 'Yes, and . . .'

Don't lose control
DO APPLY LIGHT TOUCHES TO THE STEERING WHEEL

You should always try to keep the discussion moving in a positive direction. If the appraisee seems intent on raising inappropriate issues, you may guide the conversation, for instance:

- By steering it via questions that clarify how an issue relates to their performance and their approach
- By postponing the point, offering to note down what is being said, give it some further thought or come back to it later on

Don't duck points of potential conflict
DO FACE UP TO DIFFICULTIES

Typical reasons why managers may hold back from expressing disapproval of something their staff have said or done include fears that:

- This will upset them
- They might reject the point, or, indeed, 'hit back'
- It could lead to a confrontation that will not only

ruin the conversation; but also damage their future working relationship

It is right, of course, to take all these factors into account. At some stage, however, you will probably have to disagree with something they have said or criticize their performance, perhaps on a topic they have omitted to mention.

You must consider how to present any criticism in as balanced and constructive a way as possible, giving your reasons.

Don't make generalized criticisms
DO BE SPECIFIC

Rather than making sweeping statements – 'This has been a complete disaster' – you need to highlight the particular aspects of performance that you feel strongly about. This keeps your feedback in perspective – so that the situation doesn't seem completely hopeless – and focuses discussion on the issues you want your staff member to act upon for future improvement. As before, where possible you should balance criticism with praise. For example: 'On this one, I like the way you handled A, B and C; I am rather less happy with D, E and F.'

Don't be judgemental
DO BE DESCRIPTIVE

It can be tempting to put your own inference on what the other person has said or done, characterizing your view on it in a convenient shorthand way: 'That was awful/dreadful/abysmal/terrible.' You need to concentrate instead on describing what the problem was. For example, you could explain that it:

- 'Put production back a week'
- 'Led to complaints from other staff members'
- 'Overran the available budget'

In this way you will help them to understand why the issue is one that you feel strongly about, and therefore why you have raised it. Similarly, it alerts them to possible repercussions of their future actions.

Don't talk about the person
DO TALK ABOUT THEIR BEHAVIOUR

Comments like 'You are lazy/slapdash/domineering' are not only generalized and judgemental, they also strike at the very heart of people's make-up, their personality, and their ingrained attitudes. However much you may feel such comments to be true you should avoid making your point in so personal a way, as it will only provoke a defensive reaction. People simply will not accept such comments, even if they can see they are partially true, or indeed, believe they could do anything about them. In order to make your point you should, instead, discuss the opportunities for them to:

- Increase their output – rather than be less lazy
- Attend to detail – rather than be less slapdash
- Work more closely with others – rather than be less domineering

In essence, should you ask someone to change what they **do**, they will hopefully feel there is something they can do about it. Should you ask them to change the way they **are**, however, they will feel defeated before they start.

Don't use 'irritators'
DO USE 'SOOTHERS'

In the interests of avoiding a blazing row, you may feel that you have succeeded in toning down what you really feel like saying, thus avoiding the trap of making personal attacks. Nevertheless, if you are not very careful your frustration and irritation at their behaviour may still 'leak out' and manifest itself in the use of words which will act as 'irritators'. Such words and phrases are guaranteed to provoke a defensive reaction, for instance:

- 'Can't you see . . .' – implying they are blind
- 'Didn't you hear . . .' – implying they are deaf
- 'Don't you understand . . .' – implying they are stupid
- 'I'm only being reasonable when I say . . .' – implying they are unreasonable
- 'With respect . . .' – implying the complete opposite

Phrases like these infuriate people to such an extent that they are highly unlikely to listen to what follows, however valid it may be. Similarly, if you say 'Yes, but . . .' or 'I disagree because . . .' to someone else's idea they will be so busy thinking of how to counter your objection that they will not be listening to the reasons behind it.

In order to keep them listening, and encourage them to take your points on board, you should convey criticism indirectly rather than explicitly. Make extensive use of 'soothers', phrases like:

- 'Another way of looking at this . . .'
- 'On the other hand . . .'
- 'It seems to me . . .'
- 'In my experience . . .'

You can also make extensive use of 'the royal we': 'If we take the idea you have raised, I agree that we could find . . . however, it might well result in . . . so perhaps we should look for other ways of tackling it.'

Don't pass the buck to others
DO TAKE RESPONSIBILITY FOR THE VIEWS YOU EXPRESS

In order to preserve your relationship with a staff member you may often feel inclined to say things like: 'I'm not really getting at you . . . it's just that I have had complaints'; or 'You know what this organization's like . . . and our boss insists on . . .'.

Such comments are likely to have the opposite effect to that intended, as your staff member won't take them seriously if they don't feel that you do. They may equally lose respect for you in apparently not having the courage of your own convictions. This approach is also leading you into the potentially dangerous area of commenting on other people in appraisal discussions. Furthermore, you will not be fulfilling your responsibility as a manager by being publicly disloyal to your employers.

Ultimately, you should take ownership of your viewpoint and, if you have been asked to raise points on other managers' behalves, say 'We (i.e. the management) would like you to . . .'.

Don't be dogmatic
DO EXPLORE ALTERNATIVES

However firmly held your views on a particular subject, you should not try to force other people into your own way of thinking. Nevertheless, you can, and should, explain the consequences of their not adopting your viewpoint on an issue where you are sure that you are on really firm ground. Even then, the choice is still theirs as to whether they go along with you or not.

On so many issues there really isn't just one exclusive way of viewing possible solutions to problems. Bearing in mind an earlier point of focusing on the future, rather than dwelling on the past, you should try to hold out hope for the future by being as receptive as possible to alternative ways of overcoming difficulties. After all, if you are over-committed to an approach which is subsequently proven to be unsuitable, it will be that much more difficult to change direction without feeling that this is an admission of poor judgement on your part.

Don't get bogged down
DO KEEP IT MOVING

If staff do not accept your views, you really need to find out why they are resistant to changing theirs. It could be that they feel:

- Quite happy with the way things are at present and simply unable to understand the need to change
- Resentful about being wrong-footed by this 'surprise point' that you have raised, perhaps for the first time
- Afraid of the unknown and therefore more inclined to cling to an admittedly, 'imperfect present' rather than move to an 'uncertain future'
- Inadequate now the issues have been raised, and worried about their ability to change their ways
- Suspicious about what lies ahead, particularly if they have felt manipulated in the past (once bitten, twice shy)

- Determined not to accept anything which sounds dogmatic, which they have not been consulted on, or on which they feel they are being given no room to manoeuvre.

It would be dangerous for you to make assumptions as to which of these is the case without first asking questions. Then, when you have identified the problem, you should either:

- Amend or withdraw your view if you can now see things differently – remembering the 'small steps' approach to achieving your objectives
- Ask them to accept your viewpoint as well and encourage them to try out what you are suggesting, presenting it as: 'An experiment which we will review together in a few weeks' time.'
- Postpone the issue for now and come back to it, either later in the conversation or at a later date, thus giving you both time to think about it and enabling you to move on to other, more productive, topics

Don't indulge in overkill
DO QUIT WHILE YOU'RE AHEAD

There is such a thing as giving too much feedback, however justified it may all be, and however well the conversation may have been going. At some stage your staff member will reach saturation point, unable to absorb any further points without being swamped by them. Remember that any agreed action deriving from your discussion will represent progress, and there will always be another opportunity to discuss things further when both parties have had a chance to take the existing issues fully on board.

It is better to agree a few points, which are then acted upon, then try to cover everything and find that there is no follow-through.

Don't leave things in the air
DO DRAW THE THREADS TOGETHER

This is the point at which you should recap on all the major issues discussed. There may well be common themes amongst them which allow a comprehensive summary to be made – easier for both parties to digest than a whole series of seemingly separate points. Some action plans may fit in well with others or, indeed, be interdependent. You should create 'packages' of plans in the summary which will allow your staff member to see how they are interlinked, thus providing the incentive to make them **all** work.

You will need to check that anything agreed to earlier in the discussion remains equally valid by the end. You should also prioritize points agreed for action in terms of their importance, urgency and feasibility.

You should then fix a time for both of you to review progress on agreed plans, and to come back to any unfinished or postponed business. By dealing with things in 'small packages' along the way you will find it much easier to round off the 'whole package'.

Don't leave a summary until the end
DO RECAP EVERY STEP OF THE WAY

At frequent intervals throughout the appraisal, you should pause to recap and check your mutual understanding of what has been both discussed and agreed. You can then summarize this before moving on to the next point:

'*We have agreed this, then, have we? Let's leave it for now and come back to it at the end. Can we now have a look at . . .*'

Without this constant recapping and clarifications, subsequent stages of the discussion may be based on entirely false premises that will only come to light when you attempt a summary of the entire process. By then it could be too late!

Don't forget to appraise the appraisal
DO FIND OUT WHAT THEY THOUGHT OF IT

You should check that your staff member sees the summary as a fair one. A good way of doing this is to involve them in its formulation by asking them what they feel are the main points to come out of your discussion. This will also help you to assess their understanding of – and commitment to – what has been agreed.

You should then ask them for an initial reaction to the appraisal. Do not necessary expect them to thank you for your efforts, after all they may feel you have only been doing what you are paid for. If, indeed, their reaction is negative, do not react to this. Simply note their objections and say that you would like to discuss them on a separate occasion, to help you plan for future appraisals.

Don't ever end on a downbeat
DO ALWAYS END ON A HIGH NOTE

Always take the lead and thank your staff member for their time, for all they have put into the discussion, for their honesty and, hopefully, for their co-operation. Whatever the outcome you certainly will have learnt some things about them, some things from them even, and this should have been a reciprocal process. Even if you have, on certain issues, had to agree to disagree, where the discussion has been conducted in a positive manner throughout you can still look forward to working and talking together in future.

CHAPTER 8

All things to all people

– On adapting one's approach and coping with the
unexpected

The tree that bends with the wind – survives the storm

So that's all there is to it, is it? But what about when you
come across people who are extremely negative – people
who try to take over the conversation or, alternatively,
who sit there and virtually refuse to say anything? What
about the people who just go through the motions –
seemingly agreeing with everything you say, although
you know they don't mean it? What if your frustration
has shown during the conversation and you have said
something you now regret – how do you retrieve the
situation?

Don't panic
DO KEEP CALM

When you find yourself under pressure it is vital that you
keep calm – if you are calm, you are in control. You
should therefore consider doing anything to help you
keep your cool, for instance:

- Take a few deep breaths and pause before responding
- Release tension by gripping chair arms)discreetly, of course!)
- In extreme cases find an appropriate moment to excuse yourself, and leave the room for a couple of minutes, during which you can 'cool off'

If you do find yourself losing your temper, however, simply apologize, regain your composure and try again. (You may at least get a second chance, if not a third and fourth!)

Don't give up
DO TRY A DIFFERENT APPROACH

If your 'questioning, listening, supporting and building' approach is not working, despite your best efforts and perseverence, you can try taking the lead on a few topics. Having put forward some of your views and ideas you should then pause to invite the appraisee to respond. Remember to listen attentively to what they have to say – without assuming that they will automatically agree with your viewpoint and without taking umbrage when they disagree. Once you have got them talking again you should return to the 'questioning' approach as soon as possible.

If taking the lead in this way fails to draw them back into the discussion you may find yourself having to do most of the talking. If you do have to adopt this approach it is important to present your points in terms that will be perceived positively by the appraisee. In addition to the aspects of giving feedback covered in Chapter 7, you should remember to:

- Make your points briefly – don't swamp salient points with a welter of minor detail
- Use positive words wherever you can (without this appearing too contrived or patronizing) – thus, 'difficulties' for 'weaknesses', 'challenges' for 'problems', 'developments' for 'improvements'
- Use persuasion rather than giving orders, stressing the benefits to the appraisee of following your suggestions – 'I think this will help you in the following way . . .'
- Appeal to their sense of loyalty – 'I shall be very grateful if you can try to do this . . .' or, even, 'If you don't do this, it will be letting your colleagues down'
- Offer to provide help, time and training to achieve the desired results

Also beware of the 'yes person'. It is tempting for managers to overlook a lack of commitment on the part of someone who outwardly appears receptive and enthusiastic. Do try to pre-empt them paying lip-service, by continually checking their understanding of, and commitment to, the points you have raised via extensive use of open-ended questioning.

Don't become aggressive
DO REMAIN ASSERTIVE

Remaining assertive means sticking up for your views without putting the other person's down. For example, take a situation where you have made a suggestion which has got a negative reaction from your appraisee.

First, let them see that you understand their point of view:

'I do understand your reservations about what you are being asked to do'

or, if you are getting little or no response:

'You seem hesitant, why is this?'

Then, restate your point of view:

'However, I feel that something needs to be done about this, because . . .'

Finally, keep the conversation moving forward by framing your suggestion in a way they are more likely to accept:

'So may I suggest you give it a try, then let me know if you have any problems with it.'

By keeping to this sequence of 'I do understand . . . However, I feel . . . So may I suggest . . .' – and repeating it as often as is necessary – you should be able to hold the other person's attention and give them the opportunity to follow your reasoning. They will see that you are both serious about the point you are making, and reasonable in the way you are making it. Whatever their misgivings, this approach makes it difficult for them to not, at least, give your suggestions a try.

Don't rise to the bait
DO RISE TO THE OCCASION

Should you find yourself with a staff member who responds to none of the approaches given thus far in anything other than a negative or critical way, you must resist the urge to match their response. Such hostility on their part is often instinctive and ill-considered, so you should encourage them to be specific and descriptive, to talk about behaviour rather than make personal comments:

- 'Can you give me an example of why you feel it wouldn't work?'
- 'In what way do you feel that this is unfair?'
- 'Is there anything else preventing us from doing this, do you feel?'

Don't ignore their point of view
DO SHOW YOU ARE STILL LISTENING

Where people are uptight, or upset perhaps, their views come across in a disjointed and confused way. More than ever, you will need to check your understanding of what they are saying: 'You mentioned this, now you're saying that . . . which is the more important to you?'

By doing this you are helping them to reassess their viewpoint and discover for themselves any inconsistencies and contradictions amongst their objections. Again, you should show them that you understand:

- 'I can see you feel very strongly about this'
- 'So you obviously feel very disappointed with that'

Don't hide your feelings
DO SAY HOW YOU FEEL

Tactfully, of course! You should first look to the areas of agreement, using their words as far as possible:

- 'Yes, I feel very disappointed too'

- 'I agree that mine is not the only way of looking at things'
- 'I see now that I can do more to help you with this'

Where there are areas of disagreement:

- 'As you know, I feel differently about this issue'
- 'I can't see, at the moment, how we can do what you are suggesting'
- 'With so many interruptions, I'm finding it difficult to think how we might resolve these issues'

As you can see, this does not involve being dogmatic or confrontational – 'Don't interrupt me!' Instead it merely involves saying how you feel – a subtle, but important, difference when trying to defuse potential conflicts.

Don't be sidetracked
DO STICK TO THE POINT

Concentrate purely on responding to issues directly related to the matter in hand, or things that are really hampering progress – like constant interruptions.

This will often require you to 'turn the other cheek' to unhelpful or provocative comments which would otherwise sidetrack the discussion. Where such stray comments persist you can carefully bring the appraisee back to the point by, for instance, saying: 'Could we concentrate on discussing X, I really think there is more mileage in that for us.' What this is also suggesting, is that you are looking to reach some form of agreement.

Don't settle for unsatisfactory compromises
DO AGREE ON WORKABLE COMPROMISES

Frequently, you will have to accept that the only way to reach a satisfactory resolution is for both parties to compromise. It can be tempting to settle for something that you can quickly agree on to defuse the issue, preserve the relationship and keep the appraisal moving. You may find later, however, that this 'quick fix' turns out to be an option that neither party can live with in the long term. You should, therefore, not allow yourself to be panicked into a hasty compromise.

A workable compromise requires you to consider all the available options and select whichever of these will provide the most effective solution. This can take time, but remember that there is nothing to stop you from postponing the more tricky decisions until another day. In the long run this patience will pay off.

Don't exceed your authority
DO EXPLAIN THE 'NEXT STEPS'

Where you cannot compromise – say over an issue that you know for certain (rather than 'feel for preference') has to be dealt with in its entirety, in a specific way, or by a specific date, and the staff member refuses – you may then have the right to insist. This situation should not arise very often, but when it does you must retain your professionalism in seeing it through. You must not use threats, merely indicate that you will need to take things further.

The first step is to give the staff member an opportunity to reflect on the issue after the appraisal, taking care to explain that you will also give it further consideration. You can then arrange a meeting, a few days later, to discuss it again. If they reject this offer you must explain that you will have to refer the matter to your superior, after which you will get back to them. You should also acknowledge their right to take the matter up with either their representative, your superior, or the Personnel Department, as appropriate.

Don't be despondent
DO LEARN FROM THESE EXPERIENCES

You will never be able to succeed with all of the people all of the time, no matter how well you have mastered The Perfect Appraisal. As long as you have done your best, you shouldn't feel that you have failed. Your best will continue to improve as you gain more experience, particularly in dealing with people you find difficult.

Above all, remain flexible – should one approach not work with an individual, feel free to try another one. Furthermore, having advocated the 'small steps' strategy of helping your staff to change their ways, don't forget to use it also for yourself. Gradually settle in to new approaches when developing your appraisal skills, by 'fine tuning' your behaviour rather than attempting to change your ways completely. This way you are more likely to succeed and your staff will not feel you are 'putting on an act'.

CHAPTER 9

Next Steps

– on following things through and maintaining the momentum

After all is said and done, there's a lot more said than done

A common complaint about appraisals, from managers and staff alike, is that: 'We had a good chat, but nothing actually happened afterwards!' If the 'chat' has been good, then expectations will be high on both sides and will need to be fulfilled. It is important for you to remember, therefore, that the end of the discussion is only the beginning of what appraisal is all about – positive action leading to improved future performance. This action, like any other action you take, will need careful attention if it is to proceed as planned.

Don't leave it at that
DO TAKE THE LEAD IN MAKING THINGS HAPPEN

One reason why things are often 'left at that' is probably that everyone is so very busy. After all, you will already have spent a lot of time and effort on the appraisal and will now have other things to get on with. Nevertheless, it is precisely because so much time and effort has been invested that you now need to ensure that you extract its full potential.

It can be tempting to think that enthusiasm generated by the discussion will, it itself, carry thing through to action. It may do to a certain extent but it will need some form of encouragement and you, as the manager, should take the lead in giving this encouragement.

Don't try to remember all that was discussed
DO WRITE IT DOWN

Having probably been involved in a wide-ranging and complex conversation, you cannot expect to remember everything that happened. Nevertheless, you will need to remember, at the very least for your next appraisal with that staff member. You should therefore ensure that some written record of what has taken place is produced very soon after the discussion. Furthermore, you will both need reminding from time to time of specific things that you have undertaken to do.

Don't write down everything that was said
DO HIGHLIGHT AGREED ACTION

You do not need a verbatim record of everything that was discussed. It is also not recommended that you include a scribe or tape recorder in the appraisal discussion – it is unnecessary and can be very inhibiting for both parties.

You will not even need the comprehensive minutes that are required for many meetings. What you will need to do, however, is to capture the salient points of your discussion: principal themes and views thereon; agreed action; postponed items; and any areas of disagreement. It may be enough to note most of this on your preparation form. You should, however, also produce a separate 'to do' list of 'who has agreed to do precisely what, by when'. An example of a form that can be used for this is given at Appendix 1, headed 'Action Notes'.

Don't make the report too formal
DO CONSIDER USING HAND-WRITTEN NOTES

Any notes that you make need to be presented in the same manner as what has gone before – a structured yet, in many senses, informal exchange of views and ideas between two colleagues. If your staff member discovers that the results of their appraisal are to be recorded on a formal document, this could adversely affect both the way they view the appraisal and how they participate in it. The Perfect Appraisal, remember, is not about producing 'school reports' on people.

Don't just give your version of events
DO MAKE IT A FAIR SUMMARY OF THE DISCUSSION

Some of the guidelines already given for conducting the discussion will again serve you well here. Your notes should include:

- Plenty of use of the word 'we': 'We discussed . . . We agreed'
- Emphasis of other positive words: 'Opportunities, potential, development, aims, future plans, etc.'
- Reference to all the things that you, as manager,

have undertaken to do for your staff member, as well as what they have agreed to do for you.
• Both viewpoints, in the event of any significant areas of disagreement.

It could prove useful to ask your staff member to produce their own written version of events, either as a basis for you to build on subsequently or as an interesting comparison with your own notes.

Don't forget to let them have a copy
DO GET A RESPONSE TO IT

Not only do you both need written reminders, you also need to check mutual understanding and confirm your agreement with what has been put down. You will therefore both need copies of the 'Action Plan' plus any other points to be highlighted. It is also a good idea to send your staff member a covering note – thanking them for what they have contributed to the appraisal, positively encouraging them as regards the future, and confirming any third parties whom, it was agree, should be informed of your decisions.
You should also remember to contact your immediate superior, other relevant managers, the personnel and Training Department, etc. about any relevant points for their records, or action in which they are to be involved. With all the contacts you make, you should also take care to obtain some form of response. This ensures: 'message received, understood, agreed, and acted upon'.

Don't expect the report to work miracles
DO KEEP YOUR EYE ON THINGS

Having obtained your staff member's agreement to their

involvement in the 'Action Plan' it is all too easy to sit back and let them get on with it. Two problems arise with this, however.

First, if and when they take action, you will need to monitor it. Not in such a way that they feel you are checking up on them, of course (although you are), but so that they see you are actively interested (which you should be). You should not only observe but also encourage, praise, guide and gently correct where necessary – remember, you need feedback on progress and so do they. Furthermore, you must keep notes on progress in readiness for their next appraisal.

Second, if they are not taking any action on certain things, you will also need to know – in order to do whatever is necessary to encourage this.

**Don't see any inaction as insubordination
DO OFFER HELP TO MAKE IT HAPPEN**

After all this painstaking work it is easy to become angry and frustrated if you feel that, as they are not carrying out the agreed action, they obviously:

- Only said 'Yes' to placate you
- Thought you would forget about it
- Have since changed their mind without consulting you

Before leaping in and reprimanding them it is worth considering some other possible reasons for this apparent change of heart. For example, they may:

- Simply have forgotten all about it – after all, they probably don't keep their 'Action Plan' pinned to their forehead

- Remember it in outline, but are unable to think what it was specifically that they had to do
- Know what to do, but just can't see how to go about it
- Have thought it was a good idea at the time, but it has since been overtaken by events or swamped by their other work
- Not like to come and see you about it, as they feel embarrassed and are afraid that you will react adversely

You will feel more kindly disposed to their plight if you remind yourself that you bear some responsibility for this inactivity. Whatever the cause, you obviously did not obtain their genuine understanding and commitment at the time of the appraisal – nor have you adequately confirmed it since. Perhaps you should have:

- Gone over it with them again
- Offered to demonstrate whatever was involved
- Guided them through their first couple of attempts
- Ensured that they had more time and resources to undertake the necessary action
- At least have stressed how important it was that these items did not get neglected

Don't delay
DO FOLLOW UP NEXT DAY

You may not get everything right at the appraisal discussion, but as long as you follow it up promptly – with the written report, monitoring and additional help – the appraisal will ultimately have the desired result.

Don't leave further discussion to the next full appraisal
DO KEEP TALKING TO EACH OTHER

You should frequently make time to talk with your staff.
In this way you can:

- Recognize achievements
- Explore difficulties
- Take corrective action
- Fine-tune plans
- Adjust timescales
- Pick up postponed items
- Monitor and maintain morale

Talking about work can often be just as important as
actually doing the work – how else can everyone continually improve and develop? In one form or another,
your staff will constantly be asking of you:

- 'Let me know what is expected of me'
- 'Let me get on with it'
- 'Let me know how I am doing'
- 'Let me develop my potential'

They may not always ask you this directly, of course, so
if you do not take the initiative you may miss out on
opportunities to help them give of their very best to their
working life and get the very best from it. Which is
where we came in – just one more thing to be said.

Don't rest on your appraisal laurels
DO KEEP REFINING THE PROCESS

If you have not yet started with appraisals, your best
way to begin is by involving your staff right at the

outset. You need to gain their commitment and to equip them with the appropriate knowledge and skills to take part in *The Perfect Appraisal*. Appendix 4 offers guidelines on training people for this. These guidelines will also come in useful where you already have an existing system of appraisal, helping you to use the approach of *The Perfect Appraisal* to complement current practices.

As to the future, it is important to keep looking for ways of refining and improving your approach to *The Perfect Appraisal*. After all, it is an integral part of enabling people, work – and therefore organizations – continually to develop.

OXFAM Annual Joint Review

Staff Member

To: Name ....

           Job Title ....

           Dept/Region/Area ....

Copy to: Name ....

           Job Title ....

           Dept/Region/Area ....

The purpose of this Review is to enable you and your immediate manager to take stock of how things are going for you at work – in your overall job and specific work plans, in your working relationships with other people, and any other aspects of working with OXFAM. In short, Joint Reviews – taking place throughout the organisation – are designed to promote and sustain good, productive working relationships all round.

Most jobs and people in OXFAM are developing all the time. It is therefore likely that out of this Review will emerge some points for action – by you, your manager and/or others – to help you and your work develop further over the next year.

The attached papers are provided to help you and your manager obtain maximum benefit from the

Review. Topics have been laid out to provide some talking points – but this should not prevent discussion about any other aspects of our working life. Please prepare for the Review by going through the papers. If space is insufficient please use additional sheets of paper, numbering them accordingly. A set of these papers is **also** being sent to your manager who will prepare his or her thoughts for your Joint Review.

As a result of your Review, the 'Action Notes' form should be completed along with (on the reverse side) any other agreed points which emerge from the discussion. These notes are for the benefit of yourself and your manager and would also be available to your manager's manager if required.

The other working papers will remain in the possession of you and your manager unless you both wish and agree otherwise.

If you have any queries at all about the Joint Review, do please get in touch with one of us in Personnel or Training Departments.

Preparation for Annual Joint Review
1. The Job
(a) *What are the main tasks or responsibilities in your job?*
(Please refer to the job description and note any significant changes over the last year)
(b) *Which areas of your work do you think have gone particular well during the past year?*
(Please say why you think this is)
(c) *Which areas of your work have proved most difficult during the past year?*
(Please say why you think this is)
(d) *How would you anticipate your job could develop or otherwise change over the next year?*

(Please note any items which you feel should be given priority attention)

2. Working Relationships
(a) *Who are your main work contacts?*
Please indicate where other people – within or outside OXFAM – most directly affect, or are affected by, the way you perform your job.
  (i) The ones who most directly affect the way I perform my job are:
  (ii) The ones who are most affected by the way I perform my job are:
(b) *What support and assistance with work do you receive from and/or give to others?*
(Please note instances where this works particularly well or less well)
  (i) Support and assistance received from others:
  (ii) Support and assistance given to others:
(c) *How would you like to see your working relationships change or develop over the next year?*

3. OXFAM and You
(a) *How do you feel in more general terms about working with OXFAM?*
(Please instance things about OXFAM and its work about which you feel particularly happy or unhappy)
(b) *How do you see your future with OXFAM?*
(Please indicate any particular aspirations and ambitions you have)

4. Other Aspects
Are there any other points you would like to raise that have not been covered so far?
(Please attach additional sheets as required)

5. Ideas for Action (Joint and individual)
(a) *What would you like to see done to help with things indicated above (in Sections 1–4)?*
(b) *What could you do to help things along?*

Annual Joint Review

Action Notes

This is a summary of action agreed by

(name) _____

and their manager

(name) _____

as a result of their discussion on

(date) _____

Topic	Agreed Action	Who Action, By When?

Reviewing Past Performance

Some particularly helpful questions to encourage self-assessment on the part of the appraisee and identify areas for improvement:

Introductory
What are your hopes/expectations of this appraisal?
What in particular would you like us to cover?
How do you feel in general about the past year/period?

Job
What do you see as the main purpose/responsibilities/tasks of your job?
How has the job changed/developed over the past year/period?
Which aspect of your job do you particularly like/dislike, find most/least interesting?
Which areas of your work do you think have gone well/feel pleased about?
Which areas of your work have proved demanding/difficult/disappointing/frustrating?
What do you think has brought about these achievements/caused these problems?

Relationships

Who are your main work contacts?

Who directly affects the way you perform?

Who are most directly affected by the way you perform?

What support and assistance do you receive from/give to others?

How do you feel about your working relationships with colleagues/staff/other departments/managers/me?

Personal

How do you rate yourself in terms of technical ability/problem solving/communication skills/leadership/etc.?

What skills do you have that are not being fully used in your job?

How do you feel you have changed/progressed/developed/improved over the past year/period?

How do you feel about the problem areas raised?

What would you say you have learned from these experiences?

What, with hindsight, would you do differently?

Concluding

What else would you like to raise?

What do you feel about what I have said/my assessment of the situation?

Which do you consider to be the most important/significant areas for development/improvement in the coming year/period?

Probing (Throughout as appropriate)

Go on . . .

Tell me more about . . .

Give me a typical example . . .

What	– precisely happened
	– Specifically did you do/say?
	– was the outcome?
	– else could have been done?

How	– did it arise?
	– did you handle it?
	– was it resolved?
	– often/regularly did this happen
	– important/significant do you feel it is?
	– strongly do you feel about it?
	– could it have been handled better?
	– do you mean?

| Where/When | – did this take place? |

| Who | – was involved? |
| | – else was affected/feels the same? |

| Why | – do you think this is/feel this way/say that? |

Improving Future Performance

Some particularly helpful questions to encourage the setting of targets, objectives and action plans to which the appraisee will be committed:

Introductory
How do you anticipate your job could/should develop or change in emphasis over the next year/period?
How would you like to see your working relationships develop/change?
What do you think can be done to improve things/make things even better?
Which items do you feel should be given priority attention?

Job/Relationships (For each item)
What can you do to help things along?
How will you go about it?
What help do you need from others/me?
What additional knowledge/skills would you find useful?
What training/development/special assignments would help?
What do you see as appropriate targets/objectives for

the coming year/period?
How shall we measure success/progress?
What could get in the way of success?
What could be done to overcome such obstacles?
What alternatives are open to us?

Personal
How do you see your future with the organization?
What particular career aspirations do you have?
What do you see as the next step(s) in your personal development?

Concluding
What else would you like to raise?
How do you feel about what we have discussed?
What do you see as the main targets/objectives/action plans we have agreed?
When should we meet again to review progress and plans?

Probing (Throughout as appropriate)
As on checklist of questions when 'Reviewing Past Performance', but with emphasis on the future.

Guidelines on Training for the Perfect Appraisal

These guidelines follow the format used in this book, and provide a framework for planning training modules with managers and their staff. The three modules can be taken separately or put together to form an integrated training programme.

MODULE 1

Objective: To gain commitment from participants to the idea of The Perfect Appraisal
Content Chapter 1
Structure: Introduction – What The Perfect Appraisal is, and is not, about
Group Discussion – What are the potential benefits of The Perfect Appraisal to: managers; their staff; the organization
Conclusion – Where we go from here in planning for The Perfect Appraisal
Duration: 1-2 hours, depending on time allowed for discussion throughout (the more the better)

MODULE 2

Objective: To equip participants to plan for The Perfect Appraisal

Content: Chapters 2-6

Structure: Introduction – Questions to ask ourselves when planning The Perfect Appraisal

Group Discussion – What are all the things we should take into account in answer to these questions?

Group Exercises and Discussion

– Setting objectives for an appraisal

– Planning with other people in mind

– Choosing the right time and place

– Constructing an agenda for the appraisal discussion

Conclusion – Where we go from here in conducting The Perfect Appraisal

Duration: From ½-1-day, depending on the number of exercises used and time allowed for discussion (again, the more – of both – the better!)

MODULE 3

Objective: To develop participants' skills in conducting and following up The Perfect Appraisal

Content: Chapters 7-9

Structure: Introduction – A systematic and flexible approach to conducting and following up The Perfect Appraisal

Group Discussion – What are the main skills involved in putting this approach into practice?

Group Exercises and Discussion

– Setting the scene at the appraisal

– Questioning and listening skills

– Giving and receiving feedback

– Action planning and follow-up
– Practical in conducting a full appraisal discussion
Conclusion – Where we go from here in applying our skills in The Perfect Appraisal
Duration: 1-2 days, depending on the number of exercises used and time allowed for discussion, plus practice of the skills involved (more than ever, the more the better!)

Further guidance and assistance with training for The Perfect Appraisal is available from the author, Howard Hudson, whose training consultancy is based at:
'Woodland View'
Churchfields
Stonesfield
Witney
Oxon, OX8 8PP
England